Easy Vegetarian Cooking:
100 - 5 Ingredients or Less, Easy and Delicious Vegetarian Recipes

Gina 'The Veggie Goddess' Matthews

Copyright

DEDICATION

This book is dedicated to our beloved Mother Earth, and the bountiful baskets she gifts to us. May we return these gifts, by all of us doing our part in respecting and preserving her well-being, so that our baskets may always be full.

TABLE OF CONTENTS

Chapter 3 – 5 Ingredients or Less Spinach and Greens Recipes 29

INTRODUCTION

With a passion for nature-made foods, and gardening, I've always been the one to bring 'those interesting vegetarian dishes' to potlucks, family gatherings and parties. There is a strong misconception within both the meat-eating and vegetarian community, that vegetarian eating is boring and limited. Or, on the flip-side, that cooking vegetarian meals is complicated, and you're required to obtain all these hard-to-find ingredients that are not available at most supermarkets. Well, neither misconception holds true, and that is why I decided to embark on writing a series of vegetarian cookbooks, that are user friendly for long-time vegetarians, some-times vegetarians and those who are looking to incorporate more nutritious dishes into their family's meal plans.

The '100 – 5 Ingredients or Less, Easy and Delicious Vegetarian Recipes' cookbook, marks the first book in my vegetarian cookbook series, and, I chose to go this particular route, because of the hectic lifestyle that our society leads today. Whether you're a busy mom, working professional, or time-restricted college student, the vegetarian recipes in this cookbook all require only easy to find ingredients, and easy to follow directions. The recipes are quick, easy, and, there are definitely no 'bark and berries' dishes in this cookbook. Inside, you'll find a very diverse selection of recipes, all categorized by their highlighted ingredient. This makes navigating to your favorite section and recipe, a breeze.

Along with proving that vegetarian cooking is neither boring nor complicated, the '100 – 5 Ingredients or Less, Easy and Delicious Recipes' cookbook, is also very easy on your budget. You won't need to buy any expensive, exotic, or hard-to-find ingredients. And, you also won't need to purchase any special cookware or kitchen gadgets. If you've been frustrated before with attempts at preparing vegetarian dishes, it is my desire that this cookbook changes your opinion of vegetarian cooking from one of frustration, to that of being fun, easy, and of course, fabulously delicious!

These vegetarian recipes call for a 70/30 mix of fresh ingredients, and packaged ingredients, making this vegetarian cookbook easy to follow for those who do not cook often, or, who might not acclimated to using a lot of fresh vegetarian ingredients. For the more acclimated vegetarian, any of the called-for prepared ingredients, can be easily substituted with their fresh equivalent. Many of these recipes include dairy products, so while not vegan, these ingredients can easily be swapped out with a vegan ingredient substitution

And, lastly, most recipes are not written 'in stone'. So, feel free to play around with some of the called-for ingredients, varying one or more of the vegetables, herbs or spices, or, just make them an addition to the recipe. Vegetarian cooking should not only be healthy, it should also be delicious and fun! That's coming from someone who views her kitchen, in the same way an artist of any kind, would view their art studio or office, as a place, and space, where wonderful creations, are imagined, and brought to delicious life.

Bon Veggie Appetit!

Gina 'The Veggie Goddess' Matthews

CHAPTER 1 - 5 INGREDIENTS OR LESS POTATO RECIPES

Russet Potato Recipes

Baked Seasoned French Fries

Preheat oven to 400 degrees and lightly grease a baking sheet.

Ingredients:

3 russet potatoes (cut into ¼ inch strips or wedges)

¼ cup grated Parmesan or Parmesan-Romano cheese

1 teaspoon dried basil (fresh is even better)

olive oil to drizzle

Arrange sliced potato strips in a single layer onto

greased baking sheet, skin sides down. Drizzle lightly and evenly with olive oil, and then sprinkle with Parmesan cheese and basil. Bake for 25 minutes, or until golden brown. Remove from oven, and immediately season with sea salt to taste, while fries are piping hot, and serve. Yields 2-4 servings.

Creamy Baked Scalloped Potatoes

Preheat oven to 375 degrees, and grease a 2 quart casserole dish.

Ingredients:

6 large russet potatoes, peeled and cut into small cubes (the smaller, the better)

1 can cream of mushroom soup (10.75 ounces)

1-1/4 cups milk (regular or non-dairy)

1 small yellow onion, finely chopped

½ teaspoon ground black pepper

Layer chopped potatoes and onions into casserole dish. In a bowl, stir together soup, milk and pepper, until well blended, and pour over potatoes and onions. Soup mixture should almost completely cover the potatoes and onions. If it does not, add some extra milk. Cover casserole dish with glass cover, or aluminum foil, and bake for 30 minutes. Take casserole out of oven, stir once, and return to oven to bake for an additional 30 minutes. Total cooking time is 60 minutes. Remove from oven, and allow casserole to stand for 5 minutes before serving. Yields 6-8 servings.

Grill Top Potatoes and Green Onions

Preheat your outdoor grill to high heat.

Ingredients:

6 large, already cooked, russet potatoes (cooled and cut into cubes)

4 green onions spears, finely chopped

2 tablespoons butter (regular or vegan)

Toss together cooled, cubed potatoes and green onions, and place in the center of a large piece of heavy-duty aluminum foil. Dot potatoes with butter and season with salt and pepper to taste. Tightly seal the aluminum foil around the potatoes, and cook over high heat for 20-30 minutes, or until potatoes are fork-tender. Yields 4-6 servings.

Cajun Baked Potato Wedges

Preheat oven to 375 degrees, and lightly grease a cooking sheet.

Ingredients:

2 pounds of russet potatoes, cut into wedges

2-3 egg whites, slightly beaten

2-3 tablespoons olive oil

Cajun spice blend (I like to use Mrs. Dash brand)

In a large bowl, whisk together the olive oil and Cajun spice blend. Place slightly beaten egg whites into a separate large bowl. Toss the cut potato wedges, first into the beaten egg white mixture, and then toss in the olive oil-Cajun spice mixture, taking care to coat all potatoes evenly. Arrange seasoned potato wedges in a single layer onto cooking sheet, and bake until crispy, approximately 40 minutes. Turn potatoes 2-3 times during cooking time, to ensure potatoes cook evenly. Yields 4 servings.

Velvety Cheddar Potato Bake

Preheat oven to 350 degrees, and very lightly grease a 1-1/2 quart baking dish.

Ingredients:

3 cups cooked mashed potatoes

1 can condensed cheddar cheese coup

1/3 cup sour cream (regular or vegan)

1-2 green onion spears, finely chopped

In large bowl, stir together the cooked mashed potatoes, soup, sour cream and onion, folding together until well blended. Spoon mixture into baking dish, and then bake on center oven rack for 30 minutes. Let potatoes rest for 5 minutes, season with salt and pepper to taste, and serve. Yields 6-8 servings.

Grandma's Grated Potato Dumplings

Heat a large pot of water to rolling boil.

Ingredients:

4 large russet potatoes (peeled and grated)

1 cup all-purpose flour

1 teaspoon sea salt

In a large bowl, stir together flour and salt, until combined, then toss in the grated potatoes. Stir well to thoroughly coat potatoes. Form a 'test dumpling' with a teaspoon of potato mixture. If it doesn't hold together, you can either stir in a little more flour, or add a beaten whole egg to the mixture.

Bring a large pot of salted water to a boil. Once you have your dumpling consistency to your liking, form dumplings with a teaspoon, and gently drop them, several at a time, into your pot of boiling water. Don't overcrowd your dumplings, as you want them to float freely, and, stir them occasionally with a wooden spoon, to keep the dumplings from sticking together. Reduce heat to a low boil, and continue boiling for 40 minutes. Once cooked, drain and rinse dumplings with hot water. Season dumplings with salt and pepper, and serve with butter, gravy or another of your favorite sauces. Yields 4 servings.

Rustic Potato and Arugula Salad

Bring a large pot of salted water to a boil.

Ingredients:

1-1/2 pounds russet potatoes, cut into small cubes

1 large bunch of arugula lettuce, cut into finger-torn pieces

¼ cup olive oil

3 tablespoons of either apple cider vinegar, or balsamic vinegar

1 teaspoon of minced garlic (optional)

Place cut, cubed potatoes into boiling water, and cook until just fork-tender. Do not overcook. Drain, rinse and cool potatoes. While potatoes are cooling, in a large bowl, whisk together the olive oil, vinegar and garlic. Add cooled potatoes and finger-torn arugula into the olive oil mixture, tossing gently, until all ingredients are well blended. Season dish with salt and pepper to taste. Serve immediately at room temperature. Yields 4-6 servings.

Creamy Twice Baked Potatoes

Preheat oven to 350.

Ingredients:

4 large russet potatoes

¼ cup milk (regular or non-dairy)

1 tablespoon butter (regular or vegan)

1-1/4 cups shredded Cheddar cheese (I recommend sharp Cheddar over mild for this dish)

Clean and scrub potatoes thoroughly, and pierce each potato several times with a fork. Bake at 350 degrees for 1 hour, until potatoes are soft, but firm. Remove potatoes, and let cool slightly. Once cool enough to handle, cut each potato in half, and scoop out inner potato flesh to approximately ¼ inch of the skin's edge. In a bowl, mash together the scooped out flesh of the potatoes with the butter, add salt and pepper to taste, and then evenly stuff the potato skin shells with the potato mixture. Sprinkle each filled potato with shredded Cheddar cheese, and put back into the oven to bake for an additional 15 minutes, or, until cheese is melted and bubbly. Yields 8 servings.

Sweet Potato Recipes

Easy Baked Sweet Potato Fries

Preheat oven to 400 degrees, and lightly grease a cooking sheet.

Ingredients:

8 sweet potatoes (cut into sticks or thin wedges)

1-2 tablespoons olive oil

½ teaspoon paprika

In a large bowl, whisk together the olive oil and paprika. Add cut potato sticks or wedges, and hand toss gently, until all potatoes are evenly coated. Arrange seasoned potatoes in a single layer on cooking sheet, and bake on center oven rack for 40 minutes. Remove from oven, immediately season with sea salt to taste, and serve. Yields 8 servings.

Stove Top Candied Sweet Potatoes

Bring one large pot of water to rolling boil.

Ingredients:

2 pounds sweet potatoes (peeled and cut into small cubes)

½ cup butter (1 stick) – (regular or vegan)

½ cup packed brown sugar

½ cup brandy

½ teaspoon sea salt

Add the cubed sweet potatoes to a pot of salted boiling water, and cook until tender, but firm. Do not overcook. Drain, rinse with hot water, and set aside. In a large skillet, slowly melt the butter over low heat. Once melted, slowly stir in the brown sugar, brandy and salt. Next, add in the cooked potatoes, and continuously stir and cook over low heat, until the potatoes are well glazed and heated through. Yields 6-8 servings.

Amaretto Mashed Sweet Potatoes

Preheat oven to 350 degrees.

Ingredients:

2-1/2 pounds sweet potatoes

3 tablespoons Amaretto liqueur (you may substitute pure maple syrup – grade 'A' or 'B')

¼ cup almonds (you can use slivers or thinly sliced)

pinch of ground cinnamon

pinch of ground ginger

Wash and scrub potatoes, and pierce each one with a fork several times. Place on cooking sheet, and bake in pre-heated oven until done. Approximately 1 hour and 15 minutes. Remove potatoes from oven, and let cool slightly. When potatoes are cool enough to handle, remove the skins and mash the potatoes in a bowl together with the liqueur and spices. You can mash them by hand, or use a hand-held electric mixer. Once potatoes are mashed, spoon them into a casserole dish, top with almonds, and return to oven to bake for 15-20 minutes. Remove from oven, and allow potatoes to stand for 5 minutes before serving. Yields 6 servings.

Bourbon-Baked Sweet Potatoes

Preheat oven to 350 degrees, and lightly grease a 9x13 inch baking dish.

Ingredients:

6 large sweet potatoes (peeled and cut into either thin slices or small cubes)

1 cup raw sugar

½ cup butter (1 stick) –(regular or vegan)

½ cup bourbon

½ teaspoon pure vanilla extract

Arrange cut sweet potatoes into prepared baking dish. In a medium to large saucepan, combine the sugar, butter, bourbon and vanilla extract and bring mixture to a boil over medium-high heat. Once sauce has come to a boil, remove from heat and pour evenly over the sweet potatoes. Bake on center oven rack for 40 minutes, or, until potatoes are soft. Let stand for 5 minutes before serving. Yields 8 servings.

Red Potato Recipes

Easy and Elegant Rosemary Baked Potatoes

Preheat oven to 375 degrees.

Ingredients:

6 large red potatoes (cut into wedges)

3 tablespoons olive oil

3 tablespoons melted butter (regular or vegan)

1 tablespoon chopped fresh rosemary (you can substitute dried if you don't have fresh)

In a bowl, whisk together the melted butter and olive oil and then pour into a 9x13 inch baking dish. Place cut potatoes on top of melted oil, and toss gently, until potatoes are thoroughly coated. Sprinkle potatoes with chopped fresh rosemary, and cover baking dish with aluminum foil. Bake on center oven rack for 30-40 minutes, or until potatoes are tender. You also want to stir the potatoes occasionally, to ensure even cooking. Remove from oven, season with salt and pepper to taste, and let potatoes stand for 5 minutes before serving. Yields 4 servings.

New England Creamed Potatoes and Peas

Bring large pot of salted water to boil.

Ingredients:

1 pound baby red potatoes (quartered with skin left on)

1 cup shelled English peas

1 cup milk (regular or non-dairy)

1 tablespoon butter (regular or vegan)

1 tablespoon all-purpose flour

Place cut potatoes into a pot of salted boiling water, and cook until tender, but firm. Do not overcook. Drain, rinse, and set aside. In a medium saucepan, bring 1 cup of water to a boil, add peas, and continue to cook at a low boil setting for 6 minutes, or just until tender. Drain and rinse. Using the same saucepan, melt the butter over medium heat. Once melted, stir in the flour to thicken, and then gradually whisk in the milk, stirring constantly, until entire mixture is slightly thickened. Add cooked potatoes and peas to mixture, give it a good stir, and simmer for 5-10 minutes to allow flavors to develop. Add salt and pepper to taste, and serve. Yields 4 servings.

Horseradish and Lemon Red Potatoes

Preheat oven to 350 degrees

Ingredients:

1-1/2 pounds small new potatoes (quartered and skin left on)

¼ cup butter (regular or vegan)

2 tablespoons prepared horseradish

2 tablespoons fresh lemon juice

In a small saucepan, melt butter over low-medium heat. Remove from heat, and whisk in the horseradish and lemon juice. Place cut potatoes into a 2 quart baking dish, drizzle with the seasoned butter mixture, and toss well to coat potatoes. Bake on center oven rack for 1 hour, or, until potatoes are tender. Add salt and pepper to taste and serve. Yields 4 servings.

CHAPTER 2 - 5 INGREDIENTS OR LESS BEAN RECIPES

Jalapeño Black-Eyed Peas

Ingredients:

1 can (15.5 ounce) black-eyed peas (with liquid)

½ red onion (finely chopped)

1 small can chopped jalapeno peppers (or 1-2 fresh jalapenos, finely chopped)

¼ teaspoon ground black pepper

Combine all ingredients in medium-sized saucepan, and heat on simmer for 30 minutes, while stirring occasionally, to allow flavors to fuse together. Remove from heat, add an optional garnish of fresh cilantro, and serve. Yields 2-3 servings.

Italian Green Beans in a Tomato Reduction

Ingredients:

1 pound fresh green beans (wash, trimmed and snap)

1 can (8 ounce) tomato sauce

1 can (14.25 ounce) diced tomatoes, with basil and oregano seasonings added

2 tablespoons olive oil

2 cloves fresh garlic (finely chopped)

In a large saucepan, sauté the minced garlic and olive oil over medium-low heat, until garlic becomes slightly browned. Next, stir in the diced tomatoes and tomato sauce. Give everything a good stir, cover, and continue to cook for 45 minutes to allow flavors to fuse together. Finally, stir in the green beans, and cook until tender, or done to your liking. Add sea ssalt and pepper to taste, and serve. Yields 4-6 servings.

Mediterranean Chickpea Salad

Ingredients:

1 can (15 ounce) chickpeas (drained)

½ of a red onion, finely chopped

½ cucumber (peeled and diced)

½ cup red wine vinegar

½ cup balsamic vinegar

In a large mixing bowl, combine all ingredients, and stir well. Add sea salt and pepper to taste, and serve at room temperature. This also makes a great cold picnic salad, since it doesn't contain any mayo, or other cream-based ingredients. Yields 4 servings.

Garlic-Infused Green Beans with Almonds

Ingredients:

3 cans (14.5 ounce each) French cut green beans (rinsed and drained)

1 large red onion (cut into thin slivers)

1/2 cup slivered or sliced almonds

2 tablespoons olive oil

1-2 cloves fresh garlic, finely chopped

Preheat a large skillet over medium heat. Once hot, add olive oil, onion, garlic and almonds. Stir continuously, until onions become translucent, approximately 3-5 minutes. Add in the drained green beans, stir well, and cover. Continue cooking over medium heat, for another 5-7 minutes. Add sea salt and pepper to taste, and serve. Yields 6 servings.

Middle Eastern Style Green Lentils and Rice

Ingredients:

1 cup dry green lentils

1 cup dry basmati rice

2 cups water

4 tablespoons olive oil (divided)

1 large red onion (finely diced)

Place the green lentils in a pot, and cover with the 2 cups of water. Bring to a rolling boil over high heat for 5 minutes, then cover pot with a lid, and turn off heat. In a large skillet, heat 2 tablespoons of the olive oil, over medium heat. Add the rice to the oil, and stir until rice becomes opaque and white (1-3 minutes). Once the rice turns opaque, add them into the pot of lentils and water, and turn back on the heat. Bring rice and lentil mixture back to a boil, cover, and continue to cook over medium-low heat for 5 minutes. Stir once, reduce heat further to 'low', and continue cooking with lid on until rice is tender. Usually this takes about 15-20 minutes more. Important: Don't lift lid during this last cooking phase. While lentils and rice are cooking, sauté the chopped onions in the remaining 2 tablespoons of olive oil, until they become soft and translucent. If you prefer to have your onions caramelized, continue cooking over low heat until they start to turn brown, and develop a caramel-like glaze. Once all ingredients are finished cooking, stir the onions into the lentil-rice mixture, add sea salt and pepper to taste, and serve. Yields 6-8 servings.

Chilled Italian Green Bean Salad

Ingredients:

2 cans (15 ounce each) green beans, drained (you can use either regular cut or French cut)

1 red onion (sliced into thin half rings)

1 bottle (16 ounce) of your favorite Italian-style salad dressing (I prefer Braggs brand)

Combine all ingredients in a large mixing bowl, and toss well, to mix and evenly coat all ingredients. Cover bowl with plastic wrap or a lid cover, and refrigerate for at least 1-3 hours. Flavors develop over time, so if you can make this in the morning, or even the night before, this simple recipe really 'pops' with flavor.

Chilled Coconut and Cilantro Chickpea Salad

Ingredients:

1 can (15 ounce) chickpeas (rinsed and drained)

1/3 cup shredded coconut (sweetened or unsweetened)

1/3 cup chopped fresh cilantro

1 teaspoon chopped green chili peppers

2 teaspoons lemon juice

Combine all ingredients in a large mixing bowl, and stir well, until all ingredients are well blended. Cover, and refrigerate for at least 3 hours before serving. Yields 4 servings.

Lemon-Pepper Green Beans with Almonds

Ingredients:

1 pound fresh green beans (washed and trimmed)

2 tablespoons butter (regular or vegan)

¼ cup sliced or slivered almonds

2 teaspoons lemon-pepper seasoning (I use Mrs. Dash)

Steam green beans until tender, but still firm (about 8-10 minutes), drain and set aside. In a large skillet, melt butter over medium heat. Add almonds to melted butter, and cook until lightly browned. Add in the lemon-pepper seasoning, and steamed green beans. Stir well to evenly blend ingredients, and cook over medium heat for 5 minutes. Add sea salt and pepper to taste, and serve. Yields 6 servings.

Lentils, Onions and Tomatoes

Ingredients:

1 cup dry lentils

1 quart water

3 tablespoons olive oil

1 medium red onion (finely diced)

2-1/2 cups diced tomatoes (plain, or with seasonings added to it)

In a medium saucepan, bring the 1 quart of water to a boil, and add in lentils. Reduce heat to simmer, cook for 20-25 minutes, and then drain. (this will cook the lentils to their MIDWAY point) Next, heat the olive oil in a large skilled over medium heat. Add in the diced onion, and sauté until tender, about 3-5 minutes. Mix in the tomatoes and partly cooked lentils, season with sea salt and pepper as desired, and simmer for an additional 30 minutes, or until the lentils are tender. Add an optional garnish of fresh chopped cilantro, parsley or basil, and serve. Yields 4 servings.

CHAPTER 3 – 5 INGREDIENTS OR LESS SPINACH AND GREENS RECIPES

Sauteed Spinach and Shiitake

Ingredients:

1 large fresh bunch spinach (rinsed and thoroughly drained)

1 cup fresh shiitake mushrooms (stemmed and quartered)

1 medium red onion (rough chopped)

1-2 tablespoons olive oil

½ teaspoon minced garlic

Heat the oil in a large skillet, over medium-high heat. Add in the mushrooms, onion and garlic, and sauté until vegetables are not quite done cooking.

Add in the spinach, and stir constantly over medium heat, until spinach just starts to wilt. (This will only take 1-2 minutes.) If you prefer your spinach more wilted, just sauté a minute or two longer. Add sea salt and pepper to taste, and serve. Yields 2-3 servings.

Cream-of-Mushroom Spinach

Ingredients:

2 packages (10 ounces each) frozen chopped spinach

1 can (10.75 ounce) cream-of-mushroom soup

1 tablespoon butter (regular or vegan)

¼ teaspoon minced garlic

Prepare frozen spinach as directed on package, and drain thoroughly. You want to make sure to remove as much moisture as possible. If you have a salad spinner, you can give the cooked spinach a twirl in there, to remove excess moisture. In a large saucepan, combine together the drained spinach, mushroom soup, butter and garlic. Stir well, and heat to a low boil. Immediately remove from heat, add sea salt and pepper to taste and serve. Yields 4-6 servings.

Garlic and Pepper Beet Greens

Ingredients:

2 bunches of beet greens (washed, dried, and stems removed)

½ teaspoon finely minced garlic

1-2 tablespoons olive oil

¼ teaspoon red pepper flakes

2 whole lemons (cut into quarters)

Bring a large pot of salted water to boil. Drop in beet greens, and cook until tender, approximately 2-3 minutes. Drain, and immediately immerse in ice water for a couple minutes, to stop the cooking process. Once the greens are cold, drain, dry, and coarsely chop. Next, heat the oil in a large skillet, over medium heat. Add in the garlic and red pepper flakes, stirring until they become fragrant, about 1 minute. Toss in the cooked, chopped greens, and stir well to evenly coat with seasonings. Cook just until greens are hot. Add sea salt and pepper to taste and serve. Yields 4 servings.

Creamy Pepper Jack Spinach

Preheat oven to 350 degrees.

Ingredients:

2 packages (10 ounce each) frozen chopped spinach (thawed and well drained)

6 ounces shredded pepper jack cheese

¼ cup milk (dairy or non-dairy)

Combine all three ingredients in a mixing bowl, and stir, until well blended. You may add any desired seasonings at this time, if you like. Pour mixture into a 2 quart casserole dish, and bake on center oven rack for 20 minutes, stirring once midway through cooking time. Let stand for 5 minutes, before serving. Yields 6-8 servings.

Tuscany Spinach and Pine Nuts

Ingredients:

3 pounds fresh spinach (hand torn)

2 tablespoons pine nuts

2 tablespoons olive oil

1 teaspoon finely minced garlic

¼ teaspoon ground black pepper

Wash spinach, but allow a little bit of the water, to cling to the leaves. In a pre-heated skillet over medium-high heat, whisk together the olive oil, garlic, pepper and pine nuts, and cook for 2 minutes, stirring constantly. Add in hand torn spinach pieces, and cook until spinach wilts to the degree you wish them to. Add sea salt and pepper to taste, and serve. Yields 6 servings.

Asparagus Recipes

Parmesan Asparagus Spears

Ingredients:

1 pound fresh asparagus spears (washed and stems trimmed)

¾ cup grated Parmesan cheese (you may also use a Parmesan-Romano blend)

¼ cup olive oil

1 tablespoon butter (regular or vegan)

Melt together the butter and olive oil, in a large skillet, over medium heat. Add in the asparagus spears, and cook for about 8-10 minutes, or to desired firmness. Remove asparagus from skillet, and immediately sprinkle with Parmesan cheese. Add sea salt and pepper to taste, and serve. Yields 4-5 servings.

Baked Asparagus with Brie

Preheat oven to 350 degrees, and very lightly oil a shallow baking dish.

Ingredients:

1 bunch fresh asparagus (washed and stems trimmed)

½ wheel (2.2 pounds) Brie cheese (cut into slices, or rough chopped pieces)

¼ cup melted butter (regular or vegan)

½ cup dry bread crumbs (regular or seasoned)

¼ cup toasted sesame seeds

Steam the asparagus until tender, but still firm. Drain, and place in your prepared shallow baking dish. Layer cut cheese pieces evenly over asparagus. In a small bowl, stir together the melted butter, bread crumbs and sesame seeds. Sprinkle the mixture over the cheese layer, and bake for 8 minutes. Increase oven temperature to broil, and broil, just until breadcrumbs become golden brown. Let stand for 5 minutes, before serving. Yields 4-6 servings.

Citrus Glazed Asparagus

Ingredients:

3 bundles of medium-thick asparagus (washed and stems trimmed)

½ cup orange juice

zest of 1 large orange

2 tablespoons olive oil

½ teaspoon sea salt

Toss the trimmed asparagus in a bowl with the sea salt, and then place the salt-coated asparagus into a large skillet, that has a tight-fitting lid. Add in the olive oil and orange juice, cover, and let sit for at least 1 hour, to allow flavors to infuse asparagus. When ready to cook, heat the skillet over medium-high heat, and when asparagus starts to steam, cook until tender, about 4-5 minutes. Be careful to not overcook. Transfer asparagus to a serving plate, leaving the cooking juices in the skillet. Add the orange zest to remaining liquid, and continue cooking until the juice reduces down to a glaze consistency, approximately 2-3 minutes. Pour the citrus glaze evenly over the warm asparagus, and serve. Yields 8 servings.

Grilled Asparagus and Spinach Salad

Preheat your outdoor or indoor grill to medium heat.

Ingredients:

12 fresh asparagus spears (washed and stems trimmed)

6 cups fresh spinach leaves (hand torn)

¼ cup olive oil

1/8 cup lemon juice

1/8 cup grated Parmesan cheese

Whisk together the olive oil and lemon juice, on a plate. Roll the asparagus spears, a few at a time, through the mixture to coat. Set any remaining liquid aside. Grill the asparagus spears for 5-7 minutes, until tender, turning at least once, to ensure even cooking. Remove asparagus from heat, and cut into bite-sized pieces. In a large mixing bowl, toss together the spinach, cooked cut-up asparagus pieces, and Parmesan. Drizzle with any remaining lemon juice/olive oil liquid, and toss, to coat all ingredients. Add sea salt and pepper to taste, and serve. Yields 6 servings.

Baked Parmesan and Balsamic Asparagus

Preheat oven to 450 degrees

Ingredients:

1 pound fresh, thin asparagus spears (washed and stems trimmed)

1-2 tablespoons olive oil

1 ounce fresh-shaved Parmesan or Romano cheese

¼ cup balsamic vinegar

Place asparagus on baking sheet, drizzle with the

olive oil, and gently toss to coat. Arrange in a single layer, and sprinkle with the fresh-shaved cheese. Bake for 15 minutes, or until cheese is melted, and the asparagus is tender, but still firm. Transfer asparagus to a serving dish, and drizzle with balsamic vinegar. Add sea salt and pepper to taste, and serve. Yields 4 servings.

Roasted Garlic and Thyme Asparagus

Preheat oven to 350 degrees.

1/ 4| 16

Ingredients:

3 cups of asparagus (cut into large diagonal pieces)

6 sprigs of fresh thyme (finely chopped)

2 cloves of garlic (finely minced)

2-3 tablespoons of olive oil

¼ cup Chardonnay, Chablis or other white wine

Combine all ingredients in a large mixing bowl, and toss until well blended. Next, tear off 6 large pieces of aluminum foil. Divide mixture into 6 servings, and place each serving into the center, of each piece of aluminum foil. Fold each foil packet tightly, and arrange all 6 packets on a cooking sheet. Bake for

25 minutes. Remove, and serve still in foil packets. You and your guests, can add sea salt and pepper to taste, as you open the packets. Yields 6 servings.

Broccoli Recipes

Lemon Butter Broccoli with Almonds

Ingredients:

1 head fresh broccoli (cut into florets)

¼ cup melted butter (regular or vegan)

2 tablespoons lemon juice

1 teaspoon lemon zest

¼ cup slivered or sliced almonds

In a large saucepan, steam broccoli until fork-tender, about 6-8 minutes. Drain, and set aside. In the same saucepan, whisk together over low heat, the butter, lemon juice, lemon zest and almonds. Add in the cooked broccoli, and stir well to coat. Add sea salt and pepper to taste, and serve. Yields 4 servings.

Parmesan Broccoli Rabe

Ingredients:

1 pound broccoli rabe (washed and trimmed)

1-2 cloves garlic (finely minced)

5 tablespoons olive oil

1 tablespoon grated Parmesan or Romano cheese

Bring a large pot of salted water to a boil. Cut an 'X' in the bottom of the broccoli rabe, and drop into the boiling water. Cook until tender, but still firm, approximately 5 minutes. Drain, and set aside. Heat the oil, in a large skillet over medium heat. Add in the garlic and sauté for 2-3 minutes. Stir in broccoli rabe, and continue cooking for an additional 10 minutes. Remove from heat, sprinkle with the cheese, add sea salt and pepper to taste, and serve. Yields 4 servings.

Asian Sesame Broccoli

<u>Ingredients:</u>

2 cups cooked broccoli (cut into small pieces)

1 large red pepper (cut into either large dices, or rough chopped)

1 tablespoon sesame oil (only use 1 tablespoon sesame oil, as too much will be overwhelming)

1 tablespoon olive oil

1 tablespoon sesame seeds

Heat both oils in a large skillet, over medium-high heat. Add in the cooked, chopped broccoli and sesame seeds, and cook for 2 minutes, while stirring. Toss in the chopped red pepper, and cook for an additional 2 minutes. Remove from heat, add sea salt and pepper to taste and serve. Yields 4 servings.

Roasted Garlic and Lemon Broccoli

Preheat oven to 400 degrees.

Ingredients:

2 heads broccoli florets

3 cloves garlic (finely minced)

juice of ½-1 whole lemon

2 tablespoons olive oil

In a large bowl, toss together all ingredients, EXCEPT the lemon juice. Add sea salt and pepper to taste, and arrange the coated broccoli onto a large cooking sheet in a single layer. Bake on center oven rack for 20 minutes, or until broccoli is fork tender. Transfer broccoli to a serving platter, and squeeze the lemon juice evenly over the top, before serving. Yields 6-8 servings.

Zucchini Recipes

Crispy Baked Zucchini Chips

Preheat oven to 475 degrees, and lightly grease a large cooking sheet.

Ingredients:

2 medium-large zucchini (cut into ¼ inch thick slices)

½ cup seasoned dry bread crumbs (preferably the Italian seasoned blend)

1/8 teaspoon ground black pepper

2 tablespoons grated Parmesan cheese

2 egg whites

In a small bowl, whisk together the bread crumbs, ground pepper and Parmesan cheese. In a separate bowl, lightly whisk the egg whites. Dip cut zucchini slices first into the egg whites, and then drudge through the breadcrumb mixture. Place on prepared cooking sheet, and bake for 5 minutes. Turn once, and continue cooking for an additional 5-10 minutes, or until zucchini slices are browned and crispy. Yields 4 servings.

Garlic and Mint Marinated Zucchini

Ingredients:

3 large zucchini, thinly sliced (use a mandolin if you have one)

2 cloves fresh garlic, finely minced (do not use garlic powder or salt – will not turn out same)

2 cups fresh mint leaves, finely chopped

1/3 cup apple cider vinegar

¼ cup + 1 tablespoon olive oil

In a large skillet, heat the ¼ cup olive oil, over medium heat. Add in the zucchini slices and garlic, and cook until zucchini are ala dente, while stirring continuously, about 2-3 minutes. Be careful not to overcook, as you don't want a mushy consistency. Remove zucchini from heat, and toss them in a bowl with the vinegar, mint, 1 tablespoon olive oil and sea salt and pepper to taste. Spoon mixture into a mason jar, or other container that you can keep tightly sealed, and keep in the fridge. This makes as a great 'relish', garnish or light side dish, especially for soups, sandwiches and summer cookout fare.

Asian-Infused Zucchini

Ingredients:

1 large zucchini (halved lengthwise, and then cut into 1 inch pieces)

1-2 tablespoons soy sauce

1 tablespoon butter (regular or vegan)

2 tablespoons sesame seeds

pinch of fresh minced garlic

Melt the butter in a skillet, over medium heat. Add in the cut zucchini pieces, and cook until lightly browned. Stir in soy sauce, sesame seeds and garlic, and continue cooking until zucchini is well coated and tender. Add sea salt and pepper to taste, and serve. Yields 4 servings.

Warm Zucchini 'Slaw'

Ingredients:

2 medium-large zucchini (cut into fine small pieces)

½ of any variety onion (finely diced)

1 bunch of fresh, finely chopped parsley

2 teaspoons olive oil

3 tablespoons Italian salad dressing (I use Bragg's brand)

Heat the oil in a large skillet, over medium heat. Stir in zucchini pieces and chopped onion, and cook until very tender, but not mushy. Add in salad dressing, and finely chopped parsley. Stir, and continue cooking for 1-2 minutes. Transfer into a serving dish, add sea salt and pepper to taste, and serve. Yields 4 servings.

Okra Recipes

Southern Fried Okra

Ingredients:

10 okra pods (cut into ¼ inch pieces)

1 cup cornmeal

1 whole egg, beaten (you may substitute with Ener-G egg replacer)

½ cup vegetable oil

In a small bowl, soak the okra pieces in beaten egg liquid for 10 minutes. In a medium-sized mixing bowl, add the cornmeal, and any extra seasonings you might wish to add at this time (ie. Chili powder, garlic powder, etc.). Heat the oil in a skillet over medium-high heat. Dredge the egg-coated okra through the cornmeal, until evenly coated. Carefully place okra into hot oil, and reduce heat to medium, as soon as the okra starts to brown. Continue cooking, until all of the okra are golden brown. Drain on paper towels, and serve. Yields 4 servings.

Moroccan Style Okra

Ingredients:

1 pound okra (ends trimmed and sliced into ¼ inch pieces)

1 tablespoon olive oil

1 teaspoon whole cumin seeds

½ teaspoon curry powder

½ teaspoon chickpea flour

Boil okra in a pot of salted water, for 20-25

minutes, to soften. Drain, let cool slightly, and pat dry any excess water. Heat the oil in a skillet, over medium heat. Add the cumin seeds, and once they start to swell, and turn golden brown, stir in the cooked okra pieces. Continue cooking over medium heat for 5 minutes, stirring occasionally. Gently fold in the curry powder and chickpea flour, and sea salt and pepper to taste. Cook for an additional 2 minutes. Remove from heat, transfer into a serving dish, and serve. Yields 4 servings.

Cucumber Recipes

Sweet and Tangy Creamed Cucumber Slices

Ingredients:

2 large cucumbers(peeled and thinly sliced)

½-3/4 cup mayonnaise (regular or vegan)

¼ cup milk (dairy or non-dairy)

1 teaspoon sugar

½ teaspoon apple cider vinegar

In a mixing bowl, whisk together the mayonnaise, milk, sugar and vinegar until smooth. Add in the cucumber slices, and toss to coat. Add sea salt and pepper to taste, and chill for 30-60 minutes before serving. Yields 4 servings.

Sour Cream and Dill Cucumbers

Ingredients:

2 large cucumbers (peeled and cut into quarters)

1 cup heavy cream (do not use half-and-half, as its consistency is too thin)

4 tablespoons white vinegar or sherry vinegar

1 pinch fresh or dried dill

In a large mixing bowl, whisk together the heavy cream, vinegar and dill, until well blended. You may add sea salt and pepper to taste, at this point. Place the cut cucumber pieces into either 1 larger sized serving dish, or 4 individual sized dishes, and drizzle the dill cream mixture evenly over the top of the cucumbers. Yields 4 servings.

CHAPTER 4 - 5 INGREDIENTS OR LESS PASTA RECIPES

Chilled Pasta and Veggie Salad

Ingredients:

1 package (8 ounce) shell pasta (or any other small-shaped pasta)

½ cup finely chopped cauliflower

½ cup finely chopped broccoli

½ cup finely diced red pepper

1 cup cottage cheese

Cook pasta according to package instructions, drain, and rinse with cold water. In a large mixing bowl, fold together all the veggies and cottage cheese, and stir until well blended. Add in the cooled pasta, and give another good stir to evenly coat. Add sea salt and pepper to taste, and chill for at least 1-2 hours before serving. Flavors build over time, so if you can, make this the night, or morning, before serving. Yields 4 servings.

Honey Lemon Couscous with Almonds

Ingredients:

1 package (8.8 ounce) couscous

2 cups water

¼ cup slivered or sliced almonds

1 tablespoon raw honey

2 teaspoons lemon zest

Toast almonds in a dry skillet over medium-low heat, until nuts begin to brown. Next, stir in honey, and stir to evenly coat almonds. Remove from heat, and spread mixture onto a piece of aluminum foil to cool. Once completely cooled, break into small pieces. In a medium saucepan, bring the 2 cups of water to a boil, and then stir in the couscous. Cover pot with a tight-fitting lid, reduce to simmer, and cook for 10 minutes, or until all the water is absorbed. Give it a stir once or twice during cooking. Remove from heat, add sea salt and pepper to taste, and transfer couscous to a serving dish. Top with the honey almonds bits, and sprinkle evenly with the fresh lemon zest. Yields 4-6 servings.

Italian Tomato Parmesan Pasta

Ingredients:

1 package (8 ounce) angel hair pasta

2 large tomatoes (seeded and diced)

½ cup Italian salad dressing (I use Bragg's brand)

¼ cup grated Parmesan cheese (may also use grated Romano)

Prepare angel hair pasta to package instructions, drain, and transfer into a large serving bowl. Stir in the salad dressing and tomatoes, and toss to evenly coat. Top with the Parmesan cheese, add sea salt and pepper to taste, and serve. Yields 4 servings.

Cheddar Mac and Corn

Preheat oven to 350 degrees, and lightly grease a baking dish.

Ingredients:

1 cup un-cooked elbow macaroni noodles

1 can (14.75 ounce) creamed corn

1 can (11.25 ounce) regular corn

½ cup butter, softened to room temperature (1 stick) – (regular or vegan)

8 ounces shredded sharp Cheddar cheese

In a large mixing bowl, stir together the creamed corn, regular corn, and un-cooked macaroni noodles. Using a fork, 'cut' the butter into the corn-noodle mixture, and then fold in the cheese. Give everything a good stir, to blend, and then transfer into your prepared baking dish. Cover with aluminum foil, and bake for 30 minutes. Remove foil, stir, and bake for an additional 30 minutes uncovered. Add sea salt and pepper to taste, and serve. Yields 6 servings.

Lemon-Basil Pasta

Ingredients:

1 pound spaghetti, linguini or fettuccini noodles

2 tablespoons olive oil

2 tablespoons lemon juice

1 tablespoon fresh or dried basil

Cook pasta according to package instructions, drain, and transfer into large mixing bowl. In a small bowl, whisk together the olive oil, lemon juice and basil. Pour over the hot, cooked pasta, and toss to evenly coat. Add sea salt and pepper to taste, and serve. Yields 6 servings.

Peppers and Penne

Ingredients:

1 pound penne pasta

2 tablespoons olive oil

1 red onion (cut into thin half rings)

3 large green, red, yellow or orange peppers (or a combination), cut into thin strips

3 cloves garlic (finely minced)

Prepare pasta according to directions, drain, and transfer into a large serving bowl. While pasta is cooking, heat the oil in a skillet, over medium heat. Toss in onion, peppers and garlic, and sauté until tender, about 5 minutes. Add the sautéed vegetables to your cooked penne, and toss to blend. Add sea salt and pepper to taste, and serve. Yields 4-6 servings.

Basil and Peas Pasta

Ingredients:

1 package (16 ounce) of desired pasta shape (elbows, spirals, penne and wheels work well)

1 can (15 ounce) sweet peas (with liquid)

1 bunch of fresh basil (rough chopped)

3 large green onion spears (finely diced)

¼ cup olive oil

Prepare pasta according to al dente directions, drain, and transfer into a large serving bowl. While pasta is cooking, heat the oil in a skillet, over medium heat. Add in the green onions, and cook until slightly tender. Stir in the peas, along with their liquid, and basil. Continue cooking until heated through. Remove from heat, and fold the pea mixture into your cooked pasta, and toss well to blend. Add sea salt and pepper to taste, and serve. Yields 6 servings.

Penne, Cannellini and Escarole Pasta Bowl

Ingredients:

1 package (16 ounce) penne pasta (spiral shaped pasta works well also)

1 can (15.5 ounce) cannellini beans (with liquid)

1 head escarole (rough chopped)

1 can (14.5 ounce) diced tomatoes with garlic and basil

2 cloves garlic (finely minced)

Cook pasta according to package directions, drain, and transfer into serving bowl. While pasta is cooking, combine all the remaining ingredients in a large skillet, and cook over medium heat, until heated through. Transfer cooked bean mixture into the serving bowl with the cooked penne. Stir well to blend, add sea salt and pepper to taste, and serve. Yields 8 servings.

Greek Roasted Tomato and Spinach Pasta

Ingredients:

6 ounces linguine pasta (you may also use spaghetti pasta)

1 can (14.5 ounce) fire roasted tomatoes (dice, and retain juice)

1 box (9 ounce) frozen creamed spinach (thawed)

2 cloves garlic (finely minced)

2 tablespoons olive oil

Cook pasta according to package al dente' directions, drain, and transfer to large serving bowl. While pasta is cooking, heat the olive oil in a skillet, over medium heat. Stir in the garlic and sauté for 3-4 minutes. Add in the roasted tomatoes, along with their liquid, and bring to a simmer. Cook for 1-2 minutes, before folding in the thawed creamed spinach. Cook and stir an additional 5 minutes, and then remove from heat. Add the cooked vegetable mixture, into your bowl with the freshly cooked linguine. Add sea salt and pepper to taste, toss well to evenly blend ingredients, and serve. Yields 2-3 servings.

CHAPTER 5 - 5 INGREDIENTS OR LESS VEGGIE VARIETY RECIPES

Corn Recipes

Southern Fried Corn Fritters

<u>Ingredients:</u>

6 ears freshly shucked corn ears

4 eggs (you can substitute with the equivalent of Ener-G egg replacer)

½ cup all-purpose flour

½ teaspoon sea salt

2 cups vegetable oil for frying

Remove all silk from corn, and cut raw corn from

the cob over a large bowl. Scrape any juice from the cobs into the bowl as well. Add in the eggs, flour and sea salt, and stir until mixture forms a batter consistency. Heat the oil in a large skillet, over medium-high heat. There should be enough oil to cover the fritters. If using a deep fryer, heat oil to 325 degrees. Using a large spoon, form 3-4 silver-dollar pancake-sized fritters, to fry at a time. If using a deep fryer, adjust to size of your fryer. Fry fritter for 5 minutes on each side, remove from oil, and drain on paper towels. Add sea salt and pepper to taste, and serve. Yields 6-8 servings.

Jalapeno and Pimento Corn

Ingredients:

6 ears, shucked raw corn ears (cut kernels from cob)

2 jalapeno peppers (seeded and finely diced)

1/3 cup finely diced red onions

2 tablespoons chopped pimento peppers

2-3 tablespoons butter (regular or vegan)

Melt the butter in a saucepan, over medium heat. Add in the remaining ingredients, and cook until corn is tender. Transfer into a serving dish, add sea salt and pepper to taste, and serve with an optional garnish of fresh chopped cilantro. Yields 4 servings.

Baked Corn-Stuffed Tomatoes

Preheat oven to 350 degrees, and lightly grease a 9x13 or larger inch baking dish.

Ingredients:

10 medium-sized, firm tomatoes

3-4 cups corn (canned/drained or frozen/thawed)

½ cup melted butter (regular or vegan)

¼ teaspoon fresh ground black pepper

½ teaspoon ground paprika

Slice tops off of tomatoes, and gently scoop out pulp and seeds (like you are scooping out the insides of a pumpkin). Put the scooped-out tomato pulp and seeds in a mixing bowl, along with the corn, melted butter and spices. Add sea salt and pepper as desired, and stir well, to blend the filling mixture. Fill each hollowed-out tomato with the corn mixture, and place into your prepared baking dish. Bake for 20-25 minutes, or until heated through. Yields 10 servings.

Easy Cream Cheese Corn

Ingredients:

1 large family-size bag of frozen corn, thawed

½ cup butter (1 stick) – (regular or vegan)

1 package (8 ounce) cream cheese (softened to room temperature) – (regular or vegan)

Melt the butter in a large saucepan, over medium heat. Stir in cream cheese, and keep stirring while cooking, until cream cheese is thoroughly blended with the butter. Once you get a creamy consistency, add in the thawed corn. Mix well to coat, and cook until corn is heated through. Transfer to a serving dish, add sea salt and pepper to taste, and serve. Yields 6 servings.

Buttery Garlic and Chive Corn

Ingredients:

3-4 ears of fresh husked raw corn ears (cut kernels from cob)

½ of a large red onion (diced)

1-2 cloves fresh garlic (finely minced)

1 tablespoon finely chopped fresh chives

2-3 tablespoons butter (regular or vegan)

Melt the butter in a saucepan, over medium heat. Stir in the garlic, and sauté for 2-3 minutes. Add in the remaining ingredients, and cook until corn is tender. Transfer to a serving dish, add sea salt and pepper to taste, and serve. Yields 4 servings.

Carrot Recipes

Lemon Butter and Dill Carrots

Ingredients:

1 package (16 ounce) baby carrots, raw

2 tablespoons butter (regular or vegan)

1 tablespoon fresh chopped dill

1 tablespoon fresh lemon juice

Place carrots in a saucepan, with enough water to cover. Bring to a boil, and cook for 10 minutes, or until carrots are fork tender. Remove from heat, and drain. Put drained carrots back into the saucepan, and add in the butter, lemon juice and dill. Cook and stir over low-medium heat, until all ingredients are well blended. Transfer to a serving dish, add sea salt and pepper to taste, and serve. Yields 4 servings.

Baked Brandy and Cinnamon Carrots

Preheat oven to 400 degrees, and line a square baking dish with aluminum foil.

Ingredients:

3 cups baby carrots, raw

¼ cup brandy

1 tablespoon raw honey

1 teaspoon ground cinnamon

1 tablespoon walnut oil (may substitute with macadamia, sunflower, or grapeseed oil)

In a mixing bowl, whisk together the brandy, honey, cinnamon and walnut oil. Fold in the carrots, and toss to coat evenly. Transfer into foil-lined baking dish, and bake for 30-35 minutes, or until carrots are fork-tender, but not mushy. Yields 6 servings.

Curry Coconut Carrots

Ingredients:

2 pounds of carrots, washed, peeled and cut into

small pieces

1 can (10 ounces) cream of coconut

1/4-1/2 teaspoon ground curry powder

In a large saucepan, combine all 3 ingredients, and cook over medium heat for 20-30 minutes, or until carrots are fork-tender. Transfer to a serving dish, add sea salt and pepper to taste, and serve. Yields 8 servings.

Honey-Glazed Carrots and Snow Peas

Ingredients:

2 cups diced carrots

2 tablespoons butter (regular or vegan)

2 tablespoons raw honey

½ pound snow peas, washed and trimmed

½ teaspoon cornstarch

Bring a large saucepan of salted water to a boil. Add the carrots, and cook until fork-tender, about 5-10 minutes, depending on size of the diced carrots.

While still cooking, add in the snow peas, and cook until they are a tender crisp, about 2 minutes. Remove from heat, and drain. In the same saucepan, melt the butter, and slowly whisk in the cornstarch. Return the cooked carrots and snow peas to the saucepan, add in the honey, and stir over medium-low heat, until all ingredients are well blended and heated through. Transfer to serving dish, add sea salt and pepper to taste, and serve. Yields 4-6 servings.

Maple and Marmalade Carrots

Ingredients:

3 cups baby carrots

2 tablespoons pure maple syrup, grade 'A' or 'B' (do not use pancake syrup)

2 tablespoons orange marmalade

2 tablespoons butter (regular or vegan)

2 tablespoons packed brown sugar

Place carrots in a large skillet, and pour in just enough water to cover the carrots. Bring to a boil over medium heat, and then simmer until water has evaporated, and the carrots are fork-tender. Stir in the maple syrup, marmalade, butter and brown sugar. Stir constantly over low heat, until all ingredients are well blended, and heated through. Transfer to a serving dish, add sea salt and pepper to taste, and serve. Yields 4 servings.

Squash Recipes

Sauteed Squash and Vegetables

Ingredients:

4 yellow squash, cut into small cubes

3 medium potatoes, any variety (peeled and diced)

4 medium-large tomatoes (diced)

1 medium yellow onion (diced)

3 tablespoons butter (regular or vegan)

Melt the butter in a large skillet, over medium heat. Stir in the cut squash and other veggies, and cook until tender, approximately 20-30 minutes. Stir frequently to ensure even cooking. Transfer to a serving dish, add sea salt and pepper to taste, and serve. Yields 6 servings.

Baked Brown Sugar Squash

Preheat oven to 350 degrees.

Ingredients:

2 medium-sized acorn squash, halved and seeded (creates 4 squash halves)

2 tablespoons butter (regular or vegan)

4 tablespoons packed brown sugar

Place squash halves upside down on a cooking sheet, and bake until they start to soften, about 40-45 minutes. Remove from oven, and flip over the squash halves, so that the flesh side is now facing upwards. Sprinkle 1 tablespoon of brown sugar evenly into each squash halve, and then dot ½ tablespoon of butter on top of each squash halve. Return to oven, and continue baking for an additional 30 minutes. Add sea salt and pepper to taste, and serve. Yields 4 servings.

Sauteed Lemon Dill Squash

Ingredients:

2 large yellow squash (cut into ¼ inch slices)

2 large zucchini (cut into ¼ inch slices)

2 teaspoons fresh or dried dill

¼ cup butter (1/2 stick) – (regular or vegan)

1 tablespoon fresh lemon juice

Melt the butter in a large skillet, over medium heat. Add in the sliced squash, and cook over medium-low heat for 10 minutes. Stir in the dill, lemon juice and sea salt and pepper to taste. Cook for an additional 1-2 minutes. Transfer to a serving dish, and serve. Yields 6 servings.

Cauliflower Recipes

Mashed Cauliflower and Parsnips

Ingredients:

1 head cauliflower, cut into florets

1 parsnip, peeled and cut into cubes

¼ cup milk (dairy or non-dairy)

2-3 tablespoons butter (regular or vegan)

Steam the cauliflower and parsnip until soft, about 10 minutes (time varies depending on size of the cut vegetables), and then drain. In a large mixing bowl, mash the cooked cauliflower and parsnips either by hand, or with a hand mixer. Gradually blend in the milk, butter and sea salt and pepper to taste. Transfer to a serving bowl, and serve with an optional garnish of fresh chopped parsley. Yields 6 servings.

Creamy Baked Cauliflower

Preheat oven to 375 degrees, and lightly grease a 8x8 inch baking dish.

Ingredients:

1 head of cauliflower (cored and cut into florets)

¼ cup butter (regular or vegan)

½ cup grated Parmesan cheese

1 teaspoon prepared spicy mustard

1 tablespoon mayonnaise (regular or vegan)

Steam the cauliflower until tender, and then drain. While cauliflower is steaming, in a large bowl, whisk together the mayonnaise, mustard and salt and pepper to taste. Add in the steamed cauliflower, and toss to coat all the pieces. Transfer into prepared baking dish, dot with pats of butter, and sprinkle the top with the Parmesan cheese. Bake uncovered to 30 minutes, or until cheese is lightly browned. Let stand for 5 minutes, before serving. Yields 4-6 servings.

Miscellaneous Vegetable Recipes

Roasted Bell Pepper Toss

Preheat oven to 450 degrees.

Ingredients:

4 large green bell peppers

2 Roma tomatoes, diced

2 tablespoons olive oil

1 tablespoon diced red onion

1-2 cloves fresh garlic (finely minced)

Place the peppers whole on a cooking sheet, and bake for 30-45 minutes, or until the skin is spotted black, and the peppers are soft. Turn once during cooking time. Remove from oven and allow peppers to cool for about 10 minutes. Peel off the pepper skins, remove stems and seeds, and cut into ½ pieces. Heat the oil in a large skillet, over medium heat. Stir in the onion and garlic, and sauté for about 3 minutes. Add in peppers, tomatoes and sea salt and pepper to taste. Stir well, and cook over medium heat for an additional 5 minutes. Remove from heat, transfer to a serving dish, and serve.

Yields 4 servings.

Parsley and Lemon Brussels Sprouts with Mushrooms

Ingredients:

4 cups Brussels sprouts (cut into halves)

½ pound mushrooms (any of the smaller varieties), cut into slices

5 tablespoons butter (regular or vegan)

½ cup fresh chopped parsley

1 teaspoon fresh lemon juice

Cook Brussels sprouts in salted boiling water until tender, about 15 minutes, and then drain thoroughly. Melt the butter in a large skillet, over medium heat. Add in the sliced mushrooms, and cook until lightly browned. Stir in the cooked Brussels sprouts, parsley, lemon juice and sea salt and pepper to taste. Cook for about 3 minutes, until all ingredients are well blended, and heated through. Transfer to a serving dish, and serve. Yields 6 servings.

Crispy Season Fried Parsnip Strips

Ingredients:

6 parsnips (peeled and cut into strips)

½ cup butter, melted (regular or vegan)

¼ cup all-purpose flour

½ teaspoon of your favorite seasoning blend (ie. Mrs. Dash, Cajun blend, Italian blend, etc.)

vegetable oil for frying

In a large saucepan, cover parsnip strips with water, cover pan with lid, and boil over medium-high heat until tender, about 10 minutes. Drain, and pat dry with a paper towel. In a large Ziploc bag, combine the flour and your choice of seasoning blend. Shake to mix. Dip the parsnips first through the melted butter, and then drop them into the seasoned 'shaker bag'. Gently shake to coat all pieces. Heat a shallow layer of vegetable oil in a large skillet, over medium-high heat. Oil must be hot before adding parsnips. Once oil is hot (325-350 degrees – or when oil starts to 'wave' and crackle), gently drop in your coated parsnip strips. Fry a couple minutes on each side, until golden brown. Drain on paper towels, and serve. Yields 4-6 servings.

Grilled Garlic Cabbage Wedges

Preheat your outdoor or indoor grill to medium-high heat. Aluminum foil to wrap.

Ingredients:

1 large head of green cabbage (remove outer leaves)

1-1/2 teaspoons garlic powder (or to taste)

Olive oil to drizzle

Cut cabbage into 8 even-sized wedges, and remove the core. You can either place each individual wedge on a separate piece of aluminum foil, or put them all onto one extra large piece of foil. Season each cabbage wedge with the garlic powder, and sea salt and pepper to taste. Drizzle each wedge with a bit of olive oil, and tightly seal up the aluminum foil packages. Grill for 30-40 minutes, until tender. Yields 8 servings.

Parmesan Eggplant Tomato Bake

Preheat oven to 400 degrees, and lightly grease a cooking sheet.

Ingredients:

1 large eggplant, cut into ½ inch rounds (large enough to yield 4-6 round slices)

1-2 large, firm tomatoes, cut into slices (you need equal number of eggplant / tomato slices)

¼ cup grated Parmesan cheese

¼ teaspoon garlic powder

In a small bowl, whisk together the Parmesan cheese and garlic powder. Arrange eggplant slices on your prepared cooking sheet. Sprinkle the Parmesan-garlic mixture on top of each round. Layer each round with a tomato slice, and sprinkle with additional Parmesan cheese if you desire. Bake on center oven rack, for 15 minutes. Transfer to serving platter, top with any additional garnish as desired, and serve. Yields 4-6 servings.

Foil-Grilled Mushroom, Onion and Pine Nuts

Preheat your outdoor or indoor grill to high, and lightly grease 4 large sheets of heavy-duty aluminum foil.

Ingredients:

24 fresh crimini mushrooms (wiped clean and stems removed)

4 large green onion spears (diced)

2 tablespoons pine nuts (may substitute chopped walnuts)

¼ cup olive oil

In a small bowl, toss together the diced green onion and pine nuts. Fill each mushroom cap with a pinch of this onion-nut mix. Place 6 mushroom caps, on each piece of foil, and drizzle with olive oil. Add sea salt and pepper if desired, and seal up foil to make a foil tent packet. Place the mushroom-filled packets onto your preheated grill, and cook for 20 minutes, or until mushrooms are tender. Yields 4 servings.

Southern Fried Green Tomatillos

Ingredients:

8 tomatillos (husked and sliced into ¼ inch pieces)

2 egg whites, lightly beaten

1/3 cup cornmeal

½ teaspoon of your favorite seasoning blend (ie. Mrs. Dash, Cajun blend, etc.)

vegetable oil for frying

Place egg whites in a shallow bowl. In a separate shallow bowl, whisk together the cornmeal, your choice of seasoning blend and sea salt and pepper to taste. Heat a shallow layer of vegetable oil in a large skillet, over medium heat. Dip the tomatillo slices first through the egg white, and then through the cornmeal mixture, making sure to evenly coat both sides. Wait until oil is hot, and fry tomatillos for 2-3 minutes on each side, until a nice golden brown. Tomatillos should be tender inside, but not mushy. Drain on paper towels, and serve. Yields 4 servings.

Baked Parmesan Scalloped Tomatoes

Preheat oven to 350 degrees, and lightly grease a

small baking dish.

Ingredients:

1 can (28 ounce) of diced tomatoes, drained (regular or pre-seasoned)

1 cup crushed saltine crackers

¼ cup grated Parmesan cheese (may also use grated Romano)

¼ cup butter (regular or vegan)

1 teaspoon fresh parsley (dried parsley won't yield any flavor after baking, so avoid)

In a mixing bowl, stir together the crushed crackers, drained tomatoes, sea salt and pepper to taste, as desired, and stir well, to mix all ingredients thoroughly. Transfer mixture to your prepared baking dish, sprinkle top with the Parmesan cheese, and dot evenly with the butter. Bake uncovered for 20-25 minutes. Add an optional garnish of fresh chopped parsley, and serve. Yields 4 servings.

Latin Inspired Cabbage Slaw

Ingredients:

1 large head of green or red cabbage (cut into finely shredded pieces)

2 large red bell peppers (cut into very thin julienne strips)

1 cup finely chopped fresh cilantro

½ cup olive oil

4 lemons, juiced

In a large mixing bowl, whisk together the olive oil, fresh squeezed lemon juice, and sea salt and pepper to taste, as desired. Add in your shredded cabbage, peppers and cilantro, and stir well, until all ingredients are well blended. Refrigerate for at least 2-3 hours before serving, to allow flavors to build, and for the cabbage to soften slightly. Yields 10-12 servings.

Sugar Snap Peas with Garlic and Mint

Ingredients:

¾ pound sugar snap peas

3 large green onion spears (diced)

1-2 cloves fresh garlic (finely minced)

1-2 tablespoons olive oil

1 tablespoon fresh chopped mint leaves

Heat the oil in large skillet, over medium-high heat. Add in the sugar snap peas, onion and garlic, and stir fry for about 5 minutes. Remove from heat, and transfer into a serving dish. Stir in the fresh chopped mint leaves, and sea salt and pepper to taste, and serve. Yields 4 servings.

Creamy Swiss and French Onion Vegetable Casserole

Preheat oven to 350 degrees, and lightly grease a 2 quart casserole dish.

Ingredients:

1 package (16 ounce) frozen mixed vegetables of your choice, thawed

1 can (10.75 ounce) cream of mushroom soup

1 cup shredded Swiss cheese

1 cup sour cream (regular or vegan)

1 can (6 ounce) French-fried onions

Set aside ¼ cup of the shredded cheese, and ¼ of the French-fried onions. In a large mixing bowl, combine the thawed vegetables, mushroom soup, ¾ cup of Swiss cheese, sour cream, remaining French-fried onions and sea salt and pepper to taste. Toss well to coat and blend all ingredients, and transfer into prepared baking dish. Bake uncovered for 30 minutes. Sprinkle with remaining cheese and French-fried onions, and return to oven to bake for an additional 5-10 minutes, or until cheese has melted. Yields 4-6 servings.

Garlic Grilled Artichokes

Preheat your outdoor or indoor grill to high.

Ingredients:

2 large artichokes

1 lemon, cut into quarters

3 cloves garlic (finely minced)

¾ cup olive oil

Fill a large bowl with cold water, and squeeze the juice from one of the lemon quarters into the water. Trim the tops off the artichokes, and cut in half lengthwise. Place artichoke halves in the lemon water to prevent them from browning, while you bring a large pot of salted water to a boil. Add artichokes to the boiling water, cook for 15 minutes, and then drain. Squeeze the juice from the remaining lemon quarters into a mixing bowl, and whisk in the olive oil, garlic and sea salt and pepper to taste. Using a basting brush, brush each artichoke with the seasoned oil, and place on your preheated grill. Grill for about 10 minutes, basting and turning frequently, until the tips of the artichokes become slightly charred. Yields 4 servings.

Crispy Baked Parmesan Edamame

Preheat oven to 400 degrees, and lightly grease the bottom only of a 9x13 inch baking dish.

Ingredients:

1 package (12 ounce) of frozen shelled edamame (thawed and rinsed)

¼ cup grated Parmesan cheese

2 tablespoons olive oil

Spread thawed, rinsed edamame into prepared baking dish. Drizzle top evenly with the olive oil, and then sprinkle a layer of Parmesan cheese on top. Add sea salt and pepper to taste, if desired, and bake for about 15 minutes, or until cheese is golden and crispy. Yields 4 servings.

CHAPTER 6 – 5 INGREDIENTS OR LESS RICE RECIPES

Cumin and Peas Basmati Rice

١ / ٤ / ١٦

<u>Ingredients:</u>

1 cup dry basmati rice

½ cup fresh peas (can also use frozen/thawed or canned/drained peas)

1 teaspoon cumin seeds

1-3/4 cups water

- salt

Bring the 1-3/4 cups of water to a boil in a saucepan. Add in the rice, and stir. Cover saucepan with tight fitting lid, reduce heat to simmer, and cook until rice is tender, about 20 minutes. Reduce heat to low or warm, and stir in the peas and cumin seeds. Keep saucepan covered on the warm burner for 5-7 minutes, to allow the ingredients to fuse

89

together. Transfer to a serving dish, add sea salt and pepper to taste, and serve. Yields 4 servings.

Coconut Curry Rice

Ingredients:

2-1/2 cups dry basmati rice

4 cans (10 ounces each) coconut milk (use regular, not the lite version)

1 teaspoon curry powder

½ teaspoon sea salt

Combine all ingredients into a large saucepan over medium-high heat, and bring to boil, taking care not to let the liquid boil over the pot edges. Cover pot, reduce heat to simmer, and cook for about 20-25 minutes, or until liquid is absorbed, and rice is tender. Remove from heat, transfer into a serving dish, add sea salt and pepper to taste, and serve. Yields 6-8 servings.

Cheesy Wild Rice and Chiles Casserole

Preheat oven to 325 degrees, and lightly grease a medium-sized baking dish.

Ingredients:

1 package (6 ounce) of instant long grain and wild rice

1 container (8 ounce) of sour cream (regular or vegan)

1 package (16 ounce) of shredded Cheddar cheese

1 can (4 ounce) chopped green chilis (drained)

Prepare the instant long grain and wild rice according to package instructions. Spread ½ of the cooked rice onto the bottom of prepared baking dish. In a bowl, mix together the sour cream and chiles, and carefully spread ½ of the mixture over the rice. Top with ½ of the shredded cheese, and repeat, for another layer. Bake on center oven rack for 25-30 minutes, or until cheese is nice and bubbly. Let stand for 5 minutes before serving. Yields 6-8 servings.

Peanuts and Peas Rice

Ingredients:

1 cup dry basmati rice

2-1/4 cups water

½ cup peas (can also use frozen/thawed or canned/drained peas)

½ cup dry roasted peanuts (salted or unsalted)

¼ teaspoon ground turmeric

Bring the rice, 2-1/4 cups water and turmeric to a boil, in a saucepan over medium-high heat. Cover, reduce heat, and simmer for 20-25 minutes, or until rice is tender, and liquid is absorbed. Stir in the peas and peanuts, and cook for an additional 2-3 minutes, until all ingredients are well blended, and heated through. Transfer to a serving dish, add sea salt and pepper to taste, and serve. Yields 4 servings.

Cheddar and Peppers Brown Rice

Ingredients:

1 cup uncooked brown rice

2 cups water

1 large red bell pepper (seeded and diced)

¼ of a red onion (diced)

1 cup shredded sharp Cheddar cheese

Bring the brown rice and 2 cups of water to a boil, in a saucepan over medium-high heat. Cover, reduce heat to medium-low, and continue cooking for about 50 minutes, or until liquid is absorbed. Spray a large skillet with cooking spray, and over medium heat, sauté the diced peppers and onion until tender, but firm. Stir in the cooked rice to the sautéed vegetables, and then gradually add the shredded cheese, stirring constantly to avoid clumping and sticking. Once cheese is fully melted, transfer to a serving dish, add sea salt and pepper to taste, and serve. Yields 6-8 servings.

Easy Saffron Rice

Ingredients:

1 cup uncooked long grain white rice

2 cups boiling water, divided

2 tablespoons butter (regular or vegan)

1/8 teaspoon powdered saffron

Steep the saffron in ½ cup of boiling water. In a skillet that can be tightly covered, melt the butter over medium-high heat. Stir in the uncooked rice with a pinch of sea salt. Cook, while stirring continuously, until the rice begins to absorb the butter, and turns opaque. Be careful to not brown the rice. Once the rice has turned opaque, quickly add in the remaining 1-1/2 cups of boiling water, along with the saffron-infused water, and cover. Reduce heat to low, and cook for 20 minutes, or until rice is tender and liquid is absorbed. Do NOT lift lid during cooking. Transfer to a serving dish, add sea salt and pepper to taste, and serve. Yields 4 servings.

Sweet Cinnamon, Apple and Raisin Rice

Ingredients:

¾ cup uncooked white rice

1-1/2 cups apple juice (or apple cider)

1 red variety apple (peeled, cored and diced)

1/3 cup raisins (regular or golden)

½ teaspoon ground cinnamon

In a saucepan, first combine the rice, apple juice, diced apples and raisins. Stir in the cinnamon and a pinch of sea salt. Bring mixture to a boil, over medium-high heat. Once boiling, immediately reduce heat to low, cover, and cook for 15-20 minutes, until rice is moist and liquid is absorbed. Remove from heat, transfer to a serving dish, and serve. Yields 2-4 servings.

CHAPTER 7- 5 INGREDIENTS OR LESS FRUIT RECIPES

Honey Baked Pears

Preheat oven to 375 degrees

Ingredients:

4 Bosc pears

2 tablespoons raw honey

3 tablespoons butter (regular or vegan)

dash of ground ginger (may substitute cinnamon or cardamom, depending on preference)

Peel pears, and scoop out just the bottom core. Leave stems on the pears. You may need to cut a small bit out of the bottom flesh, so that the pears will stand upright. Arrange the 4 prepared pears, bottom-sides down, into a small square baking dish. In a small saucepan, melt the butter and honey over low-medium heat, whisking continuously, to blend. Once melted, stir in the ground ginger (or your choice of spice), and immediately remove from heat. Drizzle the melted liquid evenly onto all 4 pears, and cover with aluminum foil, allowing the pear stems to poke through the foil. Bake for 1 hour, basting a few times during cooking. Yields 4 servings.

Cranberry Apple Streusel Style Casserole

Preheat oven to 350 degrees.

<u>Ingredients:</u>

1 can (21 ounce) apple pie filling

1 can (16 ounce) whole berry cranberry (do not use the jelly-style cranberry sauce)

¼ cup of butter (softened to room temperature) – (regular or vegan)

1-1/2 cups rolled oats

¾ cup packed brown sugar

In a mixing bowl, stir together the apple filling and whole cranberries, and then pour into a shallow baking dish. In a separate mixing bowl, mix together the rolled oats, brown sugar and softened butter, until mixture is well blended and crumbly. Sprinkle evenly over fruit, and bake uncovered for 40-45 minutes, until top is browned and crisp. Let stand for 5-10 minutes before serving..Yields 6-8 servings.

Refreshing Mint and Cilantro Melon Salad

Ingredients:

4 cups honeydew melon (cut into 1 inch chunks)

3 tablespoons chopped fresh cilantro

1/3 cup chopped fresh mint leaves

1 tablespoon fresh lime juice

Raw sugar or stevia to taste (optional)

Combine all ingredients in a large mixing bowl, and toss well to ensure all ingredients are well blended. Refrigerate for at least 3 hours before serving. Yields 6-8 servings.

Cranberry Orange Apple Relish

You will need a food processor for this recipe.

Ingredients:

2 pounds whole cranberries

4 large oranges (peeled, seeded and separated into segments)

* SAVE the orange peels, and scrape off the white pithy part

4 apples, peeled (cored and diced)

4 cups raw sugar

In a blender, or food processor, toss in the cranberries, orange segments, scraped orange peels, and apple dices. Pulse until well blended and mixture resembles a chunky relish. Transfer mixture into a large mixing bowl, and add in the sugar. Stir until all ingredients until well blended. Cover, and refrigerate. Can be separated into small glass jars, leaving a ½ inch head space in each jar. If you know how to can your own food, you can do that as well. This recipe makes for a great 'dressing' over your favorite rice and bean dishes, as well as a nice soft side dish for your grilled Portobello sandwiches. You can even use this as a dressing for salads. Yields 30-40 servings.

Pineapple Stuffing

Preheat oven to 350 degrees, and lightly grease a 9 inch baking dish.

Ingredients:

1 can (20 ounces) crushed pineapple (well drained)

5 slices stale white bread (cut into cubes)

1 cup raw sugar

4 eggs (can be substituted with the equivalent of Ener-G egg replacer)

½ cup butter (regular or vegan)

Cream together the sugar and butter in a deep mixing bowl. Beat in 1 egg at a time. Next, stir in the drained pineapple and bread cubes by hand, and fold gently, to mix ingredients. Transfer into your prepared baking dish, and bake for 1 hour. Let sit for 5-10 minutes before serving, to allow dressing to firm up. Add sea salt and pepper to taste, and serve. Yields 4-5 servings.

Autumn Spiced Plantains and Pineapple

Ingredients:

2 ripe plantains (peeled and cut into 1 inch rounds)

1 can (20 ounce) chunk pineapple (drained and reserve juice)

1 teaspoon ground cinnamon

¾ teaspoon ground nutmeg

vegetable oil or cooking spray for frying

In a small mixing bowl, whisk together the ground cinnamon and nutmeg. You will take a pinch at a time, to sprinkle on the fruit as you fry it. In a large skillet, heat the oil or cooking spray over medium heat. Arrange some fruit pieces in a single layer, and sprinkle with a light dusting of the cinnamon-nutmeg spice mixture. Fry for 2-3 minutes, turn fruit over, season, and fry for another 2-3 minutes on the other side. Transfer to a paper towel-lined plate, while you continue frying the rest of the fruit. Yields 4 servings.

Fruit and Yogurt Salad

Ingredients:

2 cups any variety of apples, diced (you can leave the peels on or off, to your preference)

1 cup sliced bananas

1 cup sliced fresh strawberries

1 cup chopped walnuts

1 cup vanilla yogurt (regular or vegan)

In a mixing bowl, first stir all the chopped fruit together, and then gently fold in the yogurt and walnuts. If you want to kick up the flavors even more, you can sprinkle in some ground cinnamon, orange zest or cardamom as well. Yields 4-6 servings.

Dried Fruit and Pecans Cheese Ball

Ingredients:

1 package (8 ounce) cream cheese (softened to room temperature) – (regular or vegan)

1 package (6 ounce) mixed dried fruit (chopped into small pieces)

1 cup pecans (finely chopped)

½ package (8 ounce) of shredded sharp Cheddar cheese

2 tablespoons raw honey

For best results, you want the dried fruit and pecans, to be as finely chopped as possible, almost to a completely crushed state. If you have a food processor, spice or coffee grinder, this is a great way to get them chopped finely enough. Otherwise, you can put the fruit and pecans into a large Ziploc bag, squeeze all the air out and seal, and then pound it out gently with a rolling pin. In a large mixing bowl, cream together the cream cheese and honey using a hand mixer, until well blended and smooth. Stir in the chopped fruit and shredded cheese, and mix well. Form the mixture into a ball, and roll into the chopped nuts. Refrigerate for at least 3-4 hours before serving. Yields 4-6 servings.

Strawberry Avocado Pecan Salad

Ingredients:

10-12 strawberries (stems removed and cut into slices)

1 large avocado (pitted and diced)

½ cup pecans (finely chopped)

¼ cup olive oil

2 tablespoons raw honey

In a mixing bowl, toss together the strawberry slices, avocado pieces and pecans. In a small saucepan over low heat, gently melt together the honey and olive oil. Once the honey and oil is melted, remove from heat and season with sea salt and pepper to taste, as desired. Drizzle mixture evenly over the fruit salad, and serve immediately. Yields 2 servings.

ADDITIONAL BOOKS BY AUTHOR

◆ Easy Vegetarian Cooking: 75 Delicious Vegetarian Casserole Recipes

◆ Easy Vegetarian Cooking: 75 Delicious Vegetarian Soup and Stews Recipes

◆ Natural Foods: 100 – 5 Ingredients or Less, Raw Food Recipes for Every Meal Occasion

◆ The Veggie Goddess Vegetarian Cookbook Collection: Volumes 1-4

◆ Easy Vegan Cooking: 100 Easy and Delicious Vegan Recipes

◆ Vegan Cooking: 50 Delectable Vegan Dessert Recipes

◆ Holiday Vegan Recipes: Holiday Menu Planning for Halloween through New Years

◆ The Veggie Goddess Vegan Cookbooks Collection: Volumes 1-3

- Natural Cures: 200 All Natural Fruit & Veggie Remedies for Weight Loss, Health and Beauty

ABOUT THE AUTHOR

Gina 'The Veggie Goddess' Matthews, resides in sunny Phoenix, Arizona, and has been a lover of nature, gardening and, of course, vegetarian and vegan cuisine since childhood. 'The Veggie Goddess' strongly encourages home gardening, supporting your local farmers and organic food co-ops, animal rights, and sustaining and preserving the well-being of Mother Earth.

Made in the USA
Middletown, DE
19 December 2015